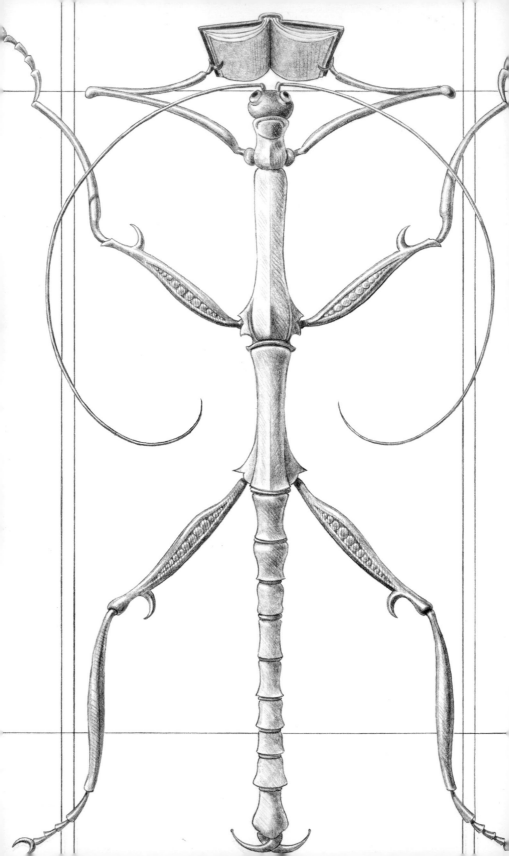

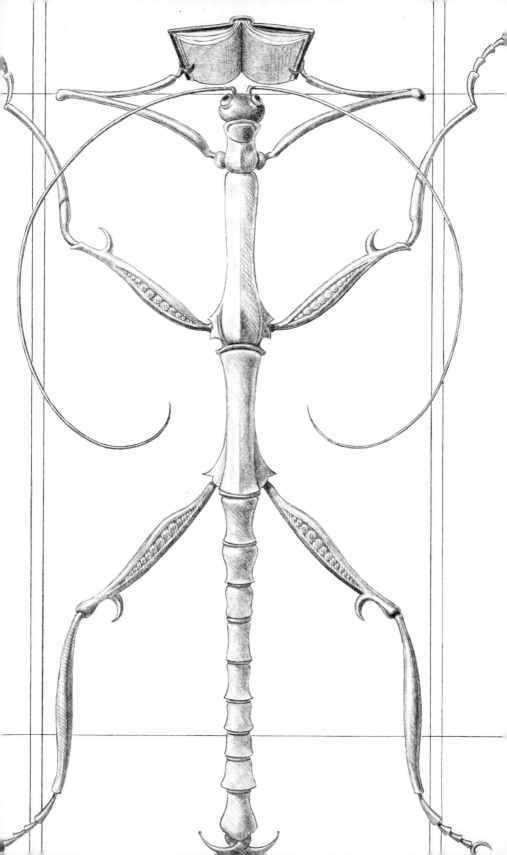

Also by Paul Fleischman

Picture Books
Time Train
Shadow Play
Rondo in C
The Birthday Tree

Novels
Bull Run
The Borning Room
Saturnalia
Rear-View Mirrors
Path of the Pale Horse
The Half-A-Moon Inn

Short Story Collections
Coming-and-Going Men: Four Tales
Graven Images: Three Stories

Poetry
Joyful Noise: Poems for Two Voices
I Am Phoenix: Poems for Two Voices

Nonfiction
Townsend's Warbler

JOYFUL NOISE
Poems for Two Voices

JOYFUL NOISE
Poems for Two Voices

PAUL FLEISCHMAN
illustrated by Eric Beddows

A Charlotte Zolotow Book

HarperTrophy®
A Division of HarperCollinsPublishers

Library of Congress Cataloging-in-Publication Data
Fleischman, Paul.
  Joyful noise.

  "A Charlotte Zolotow book."
  Summary: A collection of poems describing the
characteristics and activities of a variety of insects.
    1. Insects—Juvenile poetry.   2. Children's
poetry, American.   [1. Insects—Poetry.   2. American
poetry]   I. Beddows, Eric, 1951-   ill.   II. Title.
PS3556.L42268J69 1988   811'.54   87-45280
ISBN 0-06-021852-5
ISBN 0-06-021853-3 (lib. bdg.)

Typography by Constance Fogler

For Seth, our porch light

P. F.

*for E. H. and Echo Hill Farm with its
wonderful fireflies*

E. B.

CONTENTS

NOTE

The following poems were written to be read aloud by
two readers at once, one taking the left-hand part, the other taking
the right-hand part. The poems should be read from top to bottom,
the two parts meshing as in a musical duet. When both readers
have lines at the same horizontal level, those lines
are to be spoken simultaneously.

JOYFUL NOISE
Poems for Two Voices

Grasshoppers

Sap's rising

Grasshoppers are
hatching out
Autumn-laid eggs

Young stepping

Ground's warming

Grasshoppers are
hatching out

splitting

into spring

Grasshoppers
hopping
high
Grassjumpers
jumping

Vaulting from
leaf to leaf
stem to stem
plant to plant

leapers
Grass-
bounders

springers
Grass-
soarers
Leapfrogging
longjumping
grasshoppers.

Grasshoppers
hopping

Grassjumpers
jumping
far

leaf to leaf
stem to stem
Grass-
leapers

bounders
Grass-
springers

soarers
Leapfrogging
longjumping
grasshoppers.

Water Striders

Whenever we're asked
if we walk upon water
we answer

To be sure.

Whenever we're asked
if we walk upon water
we answer
Of course.

It's quite true.

Whenever we're asked
if we walk on it often
we answer
Quite often.

All day through.
Should we be questioned
on whether it's easy
we answer

A snap.

Should we be told
that it's surely a miracle
we reply
Balderdash!

Nonsense!
Whenever we're asked
for instructions
we always say

and do as we do.

Whenever we're asked
if we walk on it often
we answer

Each day.

Should we be questioned
on whether it's easy
we answer
Quite easy.

It's a cinch.
Should we be told
that it's surely a miracle
we reply

Rubbish!

Whenever we're asked
for instructions
we always say
Come to the pond's edge

Put down one foot

and then put down another,

resting upon the thin film
on the surface.

Believe me, there's no call
at all to be nervous

as long as you're reasonably
mindful that you—

But by that time our student   But by that time our student
no matter how prudent
has usually   has usually
                                   don't ask me why
sunk from view.   sunk from view.

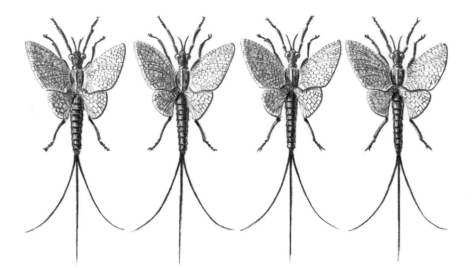

Mayflies

Your moment

               Mayfly month

Your hour

               Mayfly year

Your trifling day

               Our life

We're mayflies   We're mayflies

just emerging   just emerging

rising from the river,
born this day in May

          birthday

and dying day,

          this particle of time

this single sip of living

          all that we're allowed.

We're mayflies   We're mayflies
by the millions   by the millions
fevered

          frenzied

rushed

          no redwood's centuries
          to squander as we please.

We're mayflies   We're mayflies
swarming, swerving, swarming, swerving,
rising high

          then falling,

courting on the wing,

          then mating in midair.

We're mayflies   We're mayflies
laying eggs   laying eggs
our final, frantic act.

                              Sun's low

light's weak

                              in haste we launch them
                              down the stream.

We're mayflies   We're mayflies
lying dying   lying dying
floating by the millions

                              on the very stream

from which we sprung
so very long ago

                              this morning
back when we were   back when we were
young.   young.

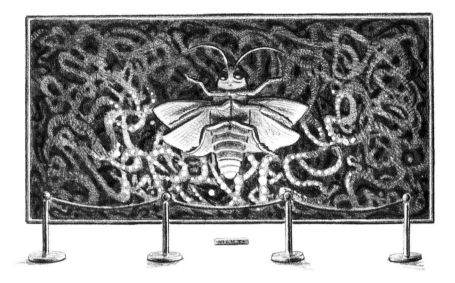

Fireflies

Light

Night
is our parchment

Light
is the ink we use

Night

We're
fireflies

fireflies
flitting

fireflies
glimmering

glowing
Insect calligraphers
practicing penmanship

Six-legged scribblers
of vanishing messages,

flickering

flashing

fireflies
gleaming

Insect calligraphers

copying sentences

Six-legged scribblers

fleeting graffiti

Fine artists in flight
adding dabs of light

Signing the June nights
as if they were paintings

flickering
fireflies
fireflies.

Fine artists in flight

bright brush strokes
Signing the June nights
as if they were paintings
We're
fireflies
flickering
fireflies.

Book Lice

I was born in a
fine old edition of Schiller

        While I started life
        in a private eye thriller

We're book lice   We're book lice
who dwell   who dwell
in these dusty bookshelves.   in these dusty bookshelves.
Later I lodged in
Scott's works—volume 50

        While I passed my youth
        in an Agatha Christie

We're book lice
attached
despite contrasting pasts.
One day, while in search of
a new place to eat

We're book lice
who chew
on the bookbinding glue.
We honeymooned in an
old guide book on Greece

We're book lice
attached
despite contrasting pasts.

He fell down seven shelves,
where we happened to meet
We're book lice
who chew
on the bookbinding glue.

I missed Conan Doyle,
he pined for his Keats

We're book lice
fine mates
despite different tastes.
So we set up our home
inside Roget's Thesaurus

We're book lice
fine mates
despite different tastes.

Not far from my mysteries,
close to his Horace

We're book lice
adoring
despite her loud snoring.
And there we've resided,
and there we'll remain,

We're book lice
adoring
despite his loud snoring.

He nearby his Shakespeare,
I near my Spillane

We're book-loving
book lice

We're book-loving
book lice
plain proof of the fact

which I'm certain I read
in a book some months back
that opposites
often are known
to attract.

that opposites
often are known
to attract.

The Moth's Serenade

Porch
light,
hear my plight!
I drink your light
like nectar

by day
Gaze in your eyes
all night
Porch light!

Porch
light,
hear my plight!

like nectar
Dream of you
by day

all night
Porch light!

I am
your seeking
circling
sighing
lovesick
knight
You are

my soul's
desire
my prize

Porch light!
My shining star!

"Keep back," they say
I can't!
"Don't touch," they say

Porch light!
Let's clasp
Let's kiss
Let's marry for a trice!

Bright paradise!
I am

seeking
circling
sighing

You are
my soul's
desire
my prize
my eyes'
delight

Porch light!

My compass needle's North!
"Keep back," they say

"Don't touch," they say
I must!

Porch light!
Let's kiss
Let's clasp
Let's marry for a trice!

(19)

Porch light!   Porch light!

Let's meet   Let's merge

Let's merge   Let's meet

Let's live for love!

For light!   For light!

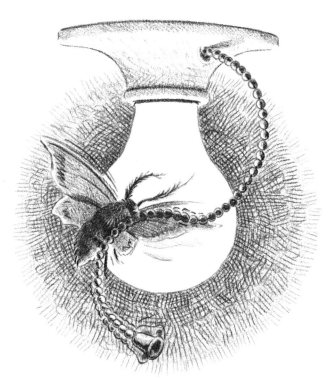

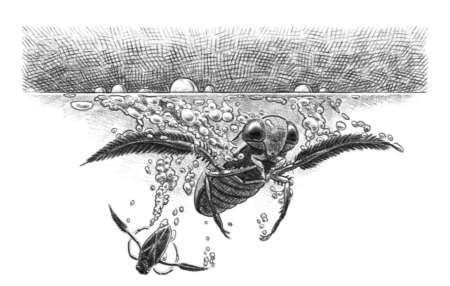

Water Boatmen

"Stroke!"   "Stroke!"
We're water boatmen
"Stroke!"   "Stroke!"
                          up early, rowing
"Stroke!"   "Stroke!"
We're cockswain calling
"Stroke!"   "Stroke!"
                          and oarsmen straining
"Stroke!"   "Stroke!"

and six-man racing shell
rolled into one.

                  We're water boatmen
"Stroke!"   "Stroke!"
worn-out from rowing
"Stroke!"   "Stroke!"
                  Bound for the bottom
"Stroke!"   "Stroke!"
of this deep millpond
"Stroke!"   "Stroke!"
                  where we arrive

and shout the order
"Rest!"   "Rest!"

The Digger Wasp

I will never
see my children,

they will never
gaze on me.

I'll have died

when they're emerging
next July.
So it must be.   So it must be.

Yet, when they
behold the home

safe and snug

I'm digging now
for their protection,

far underground,
they'll recognize
my deep affection.

they'll recognize
my deep affection.
When they hatch
and find a caterpillar,

stung and paralyzed,

left by me

for them to eat
they'll know as well
that I was wise.

they'll know as well
that I was wise.
When they learn
I'd dragged it there

in spite of every
interference,

weeds and rocks

and thieving beetles,
they'll discern
my perseverance.

they'll discern
my perseverance.
While, cocooned,

<table>
<tr><td>

safe from snow
and ice and chill,

and thank me for
my formidable
digging skill.

to climb up from their cells

and fly away
my young will
know me well.

never to be looked upon,

in replica
and know that they, in turn,
were cherished

whose face and form
they never saw.

</td><td>

they pass the winter

they'll perceive

my formidable
digging skill.
By the time they're
ready, next July,

and break the burrow's seal

my young will
know me well.
When they care
for their own children,

they'll feel my love
in replica

by the mother digger wasp
whose face and form
they never saw.

</td></tr>
</table>

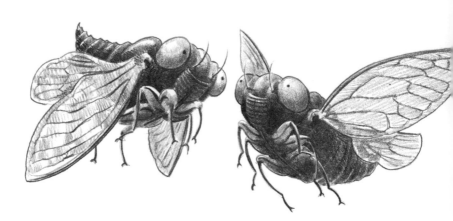

Cicadas

Afternoon, mid-August
Two cicadas singing

Five cicadas humming
Thunderheads northwestward
Twelve cicadas buzzing

the mighty choir's
assembling

Two cicadas singing
Air kiln-hot, lead-heavy
Five cicadas humming

Twelve cicadas buzzing
Up and down the street
the mighty choir's
assembling

Shrill cica-
das
droning

Ci-
cadas
droning
in the elms

Three years
spent underground

Three years

among the roots
in darkness
in darkness
Now they're breaking ground

and climbing up
the tree trunks

splitting skins
and singing

and singing
Jubilant
rejoicing
cicadas
pouring out their
fervent praise
fervent praise
for heat and light
their hymn
their hymn
sung to the sun
Cicadas

Cicadas
whining

whin-
ing

whir-
ring

pulsing
chanting from the treetops
sending
forth their
booming
boisterous
joyful noise!

ci-
cadas
whirring

ci-
cadas
pulsing

chanting from the treetops

sending
forth their
booming
joyful noise!

Honeybees

Being a bee

is a pain.

I'm a worker
I'll gladly explain.

I'm up at dawn, guarding
the hive's narrow entrance

Being a bee
is a joy.

I'm a queen

I'll gladly explain.
Upon rising, I'm fed
by my royal attendants,

                              I'm bathed

then I take out
the hive's morning trash

                              then I'm groomed.

then I put in an hour
making wax,
without two minutes' time
to sit still and relax.

                              The rest of my day
                              is quite simply set forth:

Then I might collect nectar
from the field
three miles north

                              I lay eggs,

or perhaps I'm on
larva detail

                              by the hundred.

feeding the grubs
in their cells,
wishing that *I* were still
helpless and pale.

                              I'm loved and I'm lauded,
                              I'm outranked by none.

(30)

Then I pack combs with
pollen—not my idea of fun.

               When I've done
               enough laying

Then, weary, I strive

               I retire

to patch up any cracks
in the hive.

               for the rest of the day.

Then I build some new cells,
slaving away at
enlarging this Hell,
dreading the sight
of another sunrise,
wondering why we don't
all unionize.

Truly, a bee's is the   Truly, a bee's is the
worst   best
of all lives.   of all lives.

Whirligig Beetles

We're whirligig beetles
we're swimming in circles,
black backs by the hundred.

We're spinning and swerving
as if we were on a
mad merry-go-round.
We never get dizzy
from whirling and weaving
and wheeling and swirling.

We're whirligig beetles
we're swimming in circles,
black backs by the hundred.
We're spinning and swerving
as if we were on a
mad merry-go-round.

We never get dizzy
from whirling and weaving
and wheeling and swirling.
The same goes for turning,

The same goes for turning,
revolving and curving,
gyrating and twirling.
The crows fly directly,
but we prefer spirals,
arcs, ovals, and loops.

"As the whirligig swims"

circular
roundabout
backtracking
indirect
serpentine
tortuous
twisty,
best possible
route.

revolving and curving,
gyrating and twirling.

The crows fly directly,
but we prefer spirals,
arcs, ovals, and loops.
We're fond of the phrase
"As the whirligig swims"
meaning traveling by
the most circular
roundabout
backtracking
indirect
serpentine
tortuous
twisty and
turny,
best possible
route.

Requiem

Grant them rest eternal
Maple moths
Let light undying
shine upon them.

green darners
rest eternal

Carolina sphinx moths
Grant them rest eternal

Let light undying
shine upon them.
Praying mantises

rest eternal

Black-winged damselflies

brown darners
light undying.   light undying.
Grasshoppers   Grasshoppers
great crested
                                    spur-throated

three-banded
Katydids   Katydids
                                    round-headed

northern
                                    gladiator

Cave crickets
mole crickets   Cave crickets
tree crickets   mole crickets
field crickets   tree crickets
                                    Grant them
rest eternal   rest eternal
                                    Give them
light undying.   light undying.
This past night
we had the fall's first
killing frost.

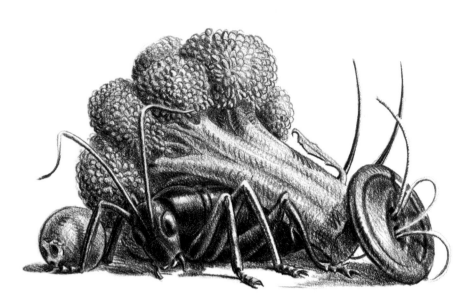

House Crickets

We don't live in meadows
crick-et
                  crick-et
or in groves

                  We're house crickets
                  living beneath
                  this gas stove
crick-et   crick-et
Others may worry

crick-et
about fall

crick-et

We're scarcely aware
of the seasons at all
crick-et
Spring, to house crickets,
crick-et
means no more

crick-et

than the time
when fresh greens
once again grace the floor
crick-et
Summer's the season
crick-et
for pie crumbs:

crick-et

peach, pear, boysenberry,
quince, apricot, plum
crick-et
Pumpkin seeds tell us
crick-et
fall's arrived

crick-et

while hot chocolate spills
hint that it's
winter outside.

No matter the month
we stay well fed and warm,

For while others are ruled
by the sun in the heavens,

we live in a world
of fixed Fahrenheit
crick-et

our unchanging

steadfast and stable
bright blue
pilot light.

No matter the month

unconcerned about cold fronts
and wind chill and storms.
For while others are ruled

whose varying height brings
the seasons' procession,
we live in a world

crick-et
thanks to *our* sun:

reliable

bright blue
pilot light.

Chrysalis Diary

November 13:

Cold told me
to fasten my feet
to this branch,

to dangle upside down
from my perch,

to shed my skin,

to cease being a caterpillar
and I have obeyed.

and I have obeyed.

December 6:

Green,

the color of leaves and life,

has vanished!

has vanished!

The empire of leaves

lies in ruins!

lies in ruins!

I study the

brown new world around me.

I fear the future.

I hear few sounds.

Have any others of my kind

survived this cataclysm?

Swinging back and forth

in the wind,

I feel immeasurably alone.

January 4:

I can make out snow falling.

For five days and nights

it's been drifting down.

I find I never tire of

watching the flakes

in their multitudes

passing my window.

The world is now white.

Astounding.

Astounding.

I enter these

wondrous events

in my chronicle

knowing no reader

would believe me.

February 12:

An ice storm last night.

Unable to see out

at all this morning.

Yet I hear boughs cracking

and branches falling.

Hungry for sounds

in this silent world,

I cherish these,

ponder their import,

miser them away

in my memory,

and wait for more.

and wait for more.

March 28:

I wonder whether
I am the same being
who started this diary.

I've felt stormy inside

like the weather without.

My mouth is reshaping,

my legs are dissolving,

wings are growing

my body's not mine.   my body's not mine.
This morning,
a breeze from the south,
strangely fragrant,

a red-winged blackbird's
call in the distance,

a faint glimpse of green
in the branches.

And now I recall
that last night
I dreamt of flying.

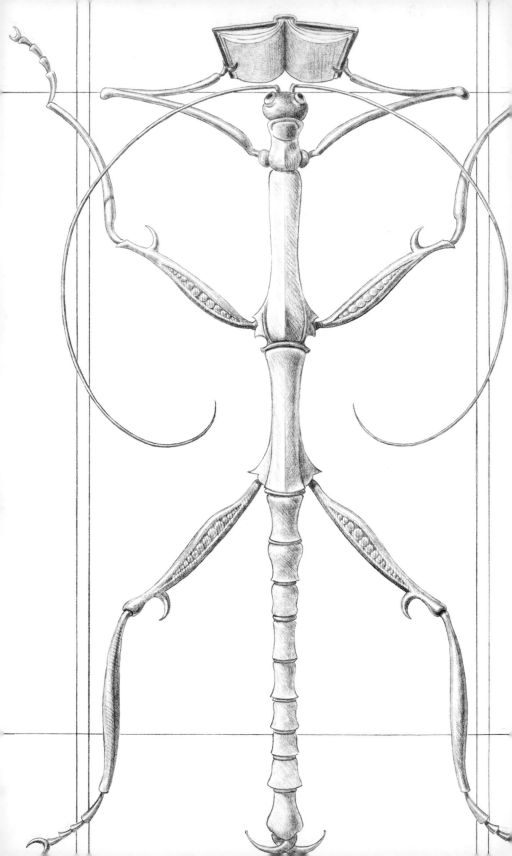